First published as :
The First Country Book
Copyright © 1974 Dinosaur Publications Ltd
The Second Country Book
Copyright © 1975 Dinosaur Publications Ltd
ISBN 0/85122/196/3
Made in Great Britain
Printed by Tabro Litho, St Ives, Cambs
Reproduction by C.L. Enterprises, Fenstanton, Cambs
Bound by J. M. Dent (Letchworth), Herts

Dinosaur Publications

The First Country Book

by Althea

Dinosaur Publications Ltd, Over, Cambridge, England

The author would like to thank Dr. Ken Joysey, Dr. Valerie Joysey and Dr. Nicholas Jardine for their help in vetting the accuracy of this book ; and Peter Merrin, Pat Scourfield, Diana Winkfield and Elsie Wrigley, who did some of the drawings ; and finally, Celia Henderson who helped get the book ready for printing.

Dinosaur Publications has published numbers of children's titles for the National Trust, and because these paperback books were so popular, I decided to do some bigger casebound books, too.

A lot of the material in this First Country Book is new, whilst the rest is a selection of some of the sections from the "All About" books.

I hope that the text and pictures are interesting and exciting for young people of all ages. I have enjoyed preparing it, and I hope you enjoy reading it.

Althea Braithwaite

Badger

Badgers' faces are white, with a broad black stripe on each side. The rest of their fur looks grey but is really made up of black and white banded hairs. The underneath part of their body is black. As they usually go out only at night, they are very difficult to see except for their faces, which are supposed to look frightening to their enemies.

They live in underground tunnels, called sets, which they dig out of the ground. They always use a tree near the entrance to clean their claws and you can sometimes find these scratched trees. They build a great many passages in their sets, and the rooms have air holes to ventilate them. Badgers are very clean animals and change their bedding

two or three times a year. When they are making a new bed, they collect a bundle of bracken and leaves and to carry it they hold it against their front legs with their heads, and shuffle backwards into their sets. Badgers are very short sighted but they have a very good sense of smell and acute hearing.

They eat anything from rabbits and hedgehogs to slugs, worms and beetles, and fruit and roots and even grass. They search out and destroy wasps' nests, and eat up the wasp grubs.

They have from two to five babies sometime between January and April. The young badgers stay with their parents until the autumn and then they go out into the world on their own.

Rabbit

There are lots of wild rabbits in this country. They like to live in groups and you can sometimes see them playing together in the fields. They eat grass and all sorts of plants, except poisonous ones, and they often do a lot of damage to crops.

They live in underground holes called burrows which they dig out of the earth. They make lots of passages and have many ways of getting in and out. The network of burrows where numbers of rabbit families live, is called a warren.

The female rabbit is called a doe, and the male is called a buck. They are usually brown in colour. Rabbits have several families every year, sometimes with seven or eight babies to look after at a time. When they are born, the babies are deaf and blind and have no fur, but in a month they are able to look after themselves.

Hare

Hares are bigger than rabbits. They have larger ears and longer hind legs. Unlike rabbits, they prefer to live by themselves, and they only live in groups during the breeding season. The female, or doe, has three or four babies in an open nest, called a form. When the babies are born they already have all their fur, and their eyes are open. Often, each baby hare lives in a separate nest by itself and the mother visits each one in turn to let it drink her milk.

If hares are very frightened, or if they get hurt, they can scream in a very alarming way.

Squirrel

Red squirrels are quite rare in the country now. Grey ones are seen much more often.

Red squirrels have reddish-brown fur, which goes rather grey in the winter. Because they love to eat pine seeds, they often make their homes in forests which have pine and fir trees. They build their nests, which are called dreys, high up in the trees. They use twigs to make the dreys.

Squirrels run up and down the tree trunks, and leap through the air from one tree to another, their bushy tails flying out behind them as they jump. Sometimes they play hide and seek with each other in the trees. When they want to pick some tasty buds or leaves, they can hang onto a branch using only their back feet, and reach out with their front feet.

Although they like to eat tree buds, nuts, bark and insects, squirrels sometimes even eat eggs and baby birds out of nests. They use their front paws like hands, and sit up on their haunches to nibble their food. They can easily cut through the shells of nuts with their sharp teeth. In the autumn they store away food in holes that they have dug, so that they have something to eat during the winter.

Squirrels have two families each year, one in the spring and another in summer. They have three or four babies each time.

Animal footprints

A good time to look for animal tracks is when snow has fallen. But you can find the marks in the soft mud by a stream or pond, too. Although some kinds of animal tracks look rather alike, they are really all different.

When the fox is creeping towards his prey, he walks with his feet close together and each foot is carefully placed one in front of the other in almost a straight line. If the tracks are in really soft mud you may even see the impression of the hairs between the pads of his feet.

The badger's feet are rather wide and you can see that its tracks overlap when it walks. This is because its rear feet step onto the tracks made by its front feet.

Otters have quite big feet, and sometimes, if the track is a clear one, you will see marks of the webbed toes. The otter has webbed feet because it needs to swim to catch its food.

When rabbits hop, they put their front paws together and their two big rear feet on each side of the front ones. When they run, the marks are much further apart and the rear tracks are smaller than usual.

The little wood mouse has feet of different sizes too. Its rear feet are much larger than its front ones.

The grey squirrel also has different sized feet. If you look closely you will notice that the rear feet look rather like little hands. They have five toes, but the front feet have only four toes each.

The small drawings show some of the tracks to look for. They are not the right size, but if you turn the page over you will find full-sized tracks of many of the different animals, showing front and rear footprints.

FOX   OTTER

BADGER

GREY
SQUIRREL

RABBIT   WOOD MOUSE

Animal Tracks

WATER SHREW

r   f

f

r

WATER VOLE

r

f

f

HARVEST MOUSE

f

f

WOOD MOUSE

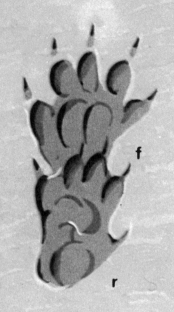

f

r

HEDGEHOG

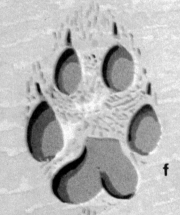

f

FOX

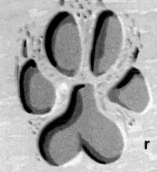

r

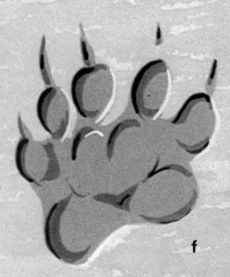

f

BADGER

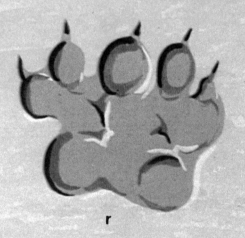

r

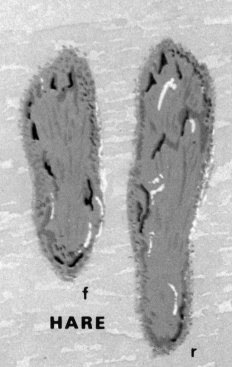

f

r

HARE

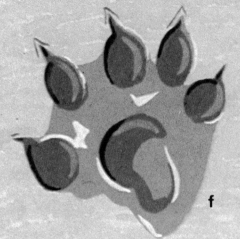

OTTER

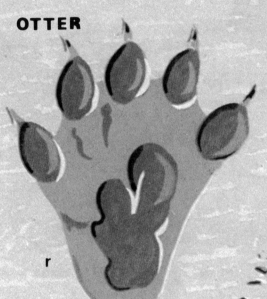

r

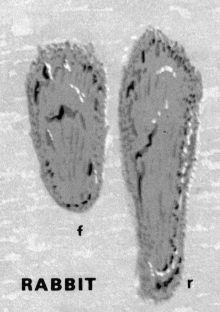

f

r

RABBIT

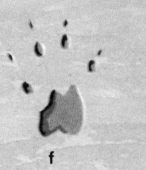

f

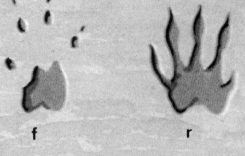

r

GREY SQUIRREL

f

r

STOAT

f

r

f

r

MOLE

f

r

WEASEL

Otter

Otters have thick brown fur which is partly waterproof, so they don't get very wet when they are swimming. To stop water getting into their nostrils and ears they close them up when they swim under water ! They have short legs and their toes are webbed to make swimming easier.

They eat fish and frogs, and even small mammals such as rabbits. Sometimes they hunt in pairs and get a lot of fun out of chasing fish and cornering them in a pool. They bark when they get excited, and can also make a whistling noise to warn other otters when there is danger.

Otters seem to have only one litter of cubs a year. There are usually two to four cubs, and when they are about eight weeks old their parents teach them to swim. They live for about 15 years.

Because otters are so shy, you will be lucky if you ever see one. Some people have been lucky enough to keep them as pets, and if you want to know more about them there is a marvellous book worth reading called 'Ring of Bright Water' by Gavin Maxwell.

Heron

Herons are wading birds with long legs and dagger-shaped beaks. They often stand very still for a long time in shallow water or on the bank, waiting patiently to pounce on a fish or perhaps a young rat.

Herons nest in noisy colonies in the tops of tall trees, such as elms or oaks. They make large flat nests, and they lay three or four bluish-green eggs. Both male and female birds take turns to sit on the nest until the eggs hatch out. They return to the same nesting colony every year.

Freshwater Fish

All the fishes shown on the next page can be found in different parts of this country.

Salmon The salmon is a large fish which lives mainly in salt water except when it swims up-river to breed. You may be lucky enough to see them leaping up over high waterfalls on their journey.

Bream The bream is a handsome bronze coloured fish. He prefers to live in slow-flowing or stagnant waters. He is sociable and likes to spend his time with other fish.

Perch The perch is a very colourful fish and is often found near reeds or large stones. He eats most kinds of small fish, and he is particularly fond of sticklebacks. You can see him chasing them in the picture.

Trout You can sometimes see trout rising to the surface of the water looking for the insects they eat. They can grow quite large and some of the biggest are found in the lochs and rivers of Scotland.

Stickleback The sticklebacks in the picture will have to move fast or the perch will catch them and eat them up ! The lower fish is the male. He is a brilliant red colour underneath to attract females during the breeding season.

Pike The pike is a very large fish with a long body. He often lurks in weedy shallows hoping to catch and eat small fish. He is one of the fiercest fish in the river.

Loach The loach is quite small and he lives under stones on the riverbed. He is well disguised because he is the same colour as the stones and can't be seen by the large fish like pike which love to eat loach.

Trout

Bream

Salmon

Perch

Stickleback

ike

Loach

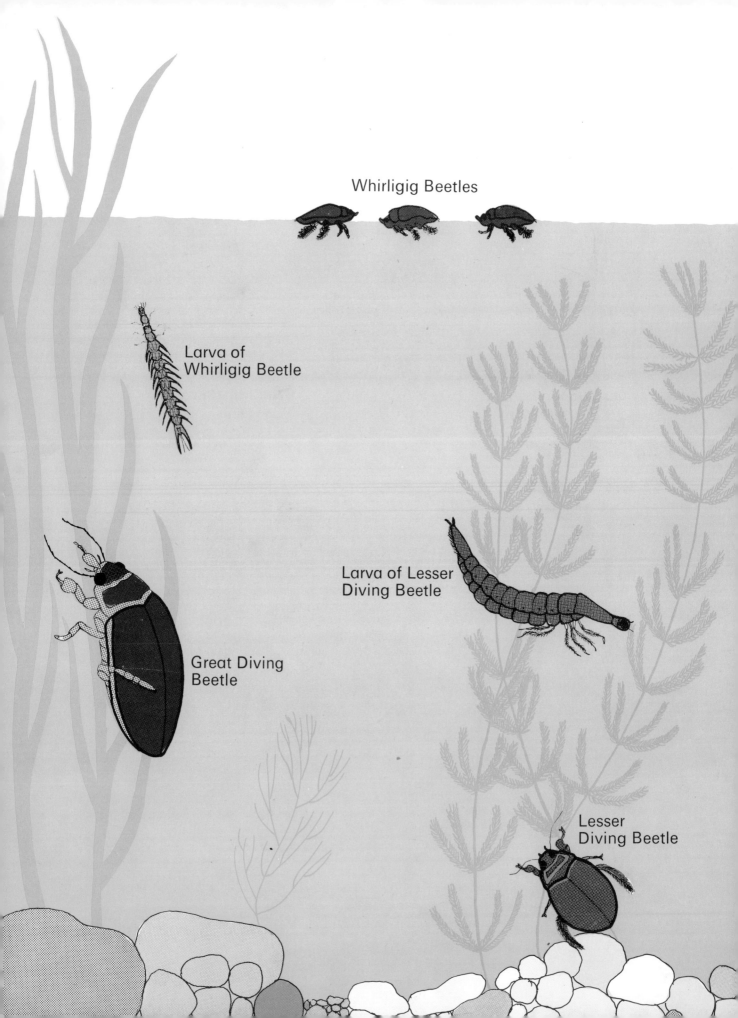

Whirligig Beetles

Larva of
Whirligig Beetle

Larva of Lesser
Diving Beetle

Great Diving
Beetle

Lesser
Diving Beetle

Water Beetles

Water beetles breathe air just like land insects. Although some of them can fly, they spend most of their time under water. They store air under their wing covers, and they breathe it as they swim. The trapped air makes them very light, so as soon as they stop swimming they float to the surface without any effort.

They use their jaws and their front legs to catch and hold their food, and they eat insects as well as water plants. If they don't want to float to the surface they use their middle legs to cling on to weeds or stones. Their back legs, which are fringed with a line of stiff hairs, are used for swimming.

Water beetles lay eggs which hatch out into larvae, and you can see two of these in the illustration. Some kinds of water beetle have larvae which when fully grown, crawl out of the pond and bury themselves in the mud, where each turns into a pupa. Later the new beetle scuttles back into the water.

There are lots of different kinds of water beetle. One particularly funny one is called a Whirligig beetle. This has a broad flat body and wide back legs and swims round and round in circles on the surface of the water. Luckily, they never seem to bump into each other! If they are frightened they quickly dive under the surface of the water to safety.

Strange Water Creatures

Lots of other strange creatures live in ponds. Because they can fly, *Waterboatmen* often travel from pond to pond in this way. They have extremely long hind legs which they use as oars, and the Greater Waterboatmen swim around on their backs. Sometimes you can see *Pond Skaters* and *Water Measurers* with their long legs, who seem to skate or slide over the water. They are supported by the invisible skin which is on the surface of all water. The velvety hair on the underneath of their bodies stops them from getting wet.

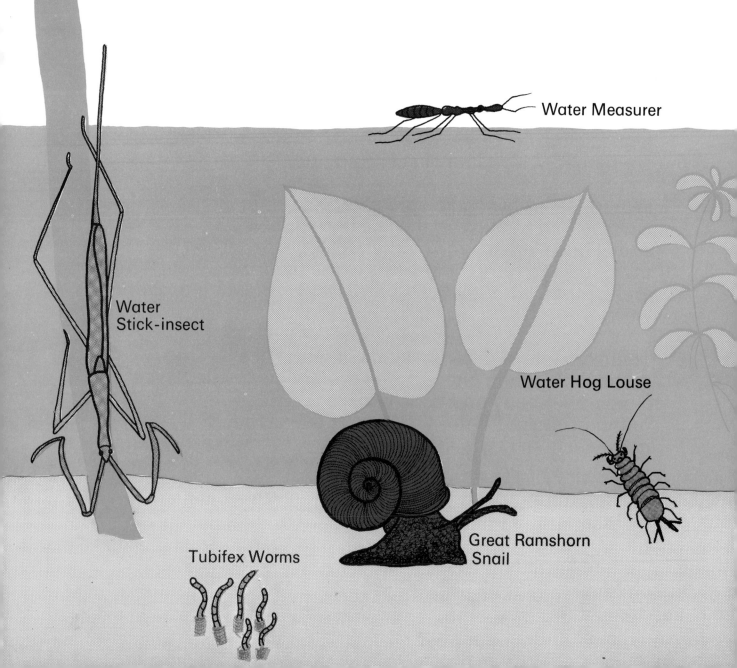

Water Measurer

Water Stick-insect

Water Hog Louse

Tubifex Worms

Great Ramshorn Snail

On the bottom of the pond live some strange looking worms. The *Tubifex* gets his name because he builds himself a tube of mud to live in. Another worm who shares the bed of the pond is the *Flatworm.* You might see a *Freshwater Louse* whose land cousin is the woodlouse. You can usually find several types of snail in ponds too. They eat the smaller water plants and they help to keep the water clean. They have to come up to the surface to breathe air every so often.

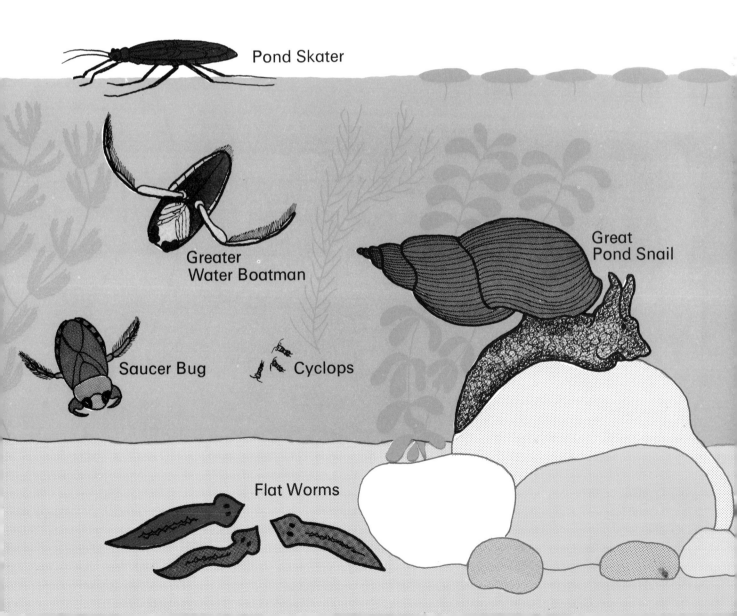

Pond Skater

Greater
Water Boatman

Saucer Bug

Cyclops

Great
Pond Snail

Flat Worms

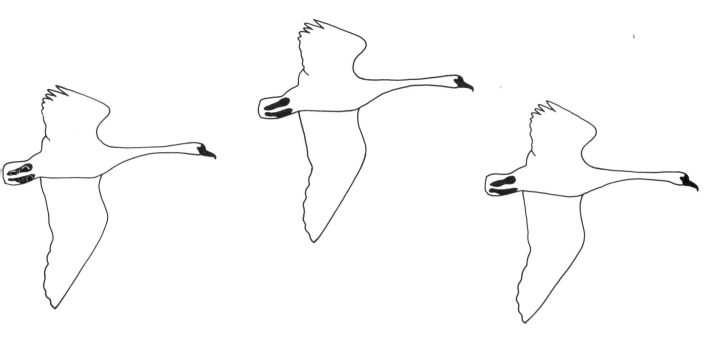

Swan

The Mute Swan is called mute because it doesn't say very much. Swans are very sociable and, except during the breeding season, they often live in large herds. When a swan chooses a mate they stay together for the whole of their lives. They always return to the same nesting site each year, where they make very large untidy nests, using rushes and grass. After laying about eight greenish-white eggs, the female sits on them while the male guards her, fiercely chasing off any other birds or people who come too near.

When the babies are hatched they are taken out onto the water. If the mother swan is worried about her children's safety she lets them scramble up onto her back, holding her foot out to make a step for them to climb up. When they return to the nest after an outing she carefully cleans them with her beak.

Young swans are called cygnets, and at first they are a brownish colour. But when they are two years old they change into pure white adult swans.

Coot and Moorhen

Coots are larger than moorhens, and it's very easy to tell the difference because the coot has a white beak and a white patch on the front of his head, while the moorhen has a red patch and a red beak with a yellow tip. Both birds have long green legs, and when they swim, their heads bob up and down in rhythm with their feet. They can swim well underneath the water too, but the moorhen usually only dives when it is alarmed, and feeds mainly on the surface. Coots are fun to watch as they dive down to find insects and plants and then bob up again in another place.

Moorhens have as many as three families each season. They are able to swim as soon as they are born, and the older youngsters often help to look after the babies.

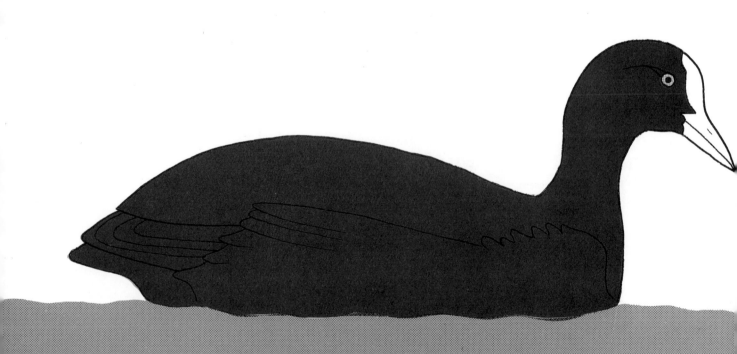

From spawn to frog

Common frogs always lay their eggs in fresh water. At first the eggs sink to the bottom. Then the jelly which covers each egg to protect it swells up, and the eggs float to the surface. The female frog sometimes lays as many as four thousand eggs, and the mass of eggs covered by jelly is called frog spawn.

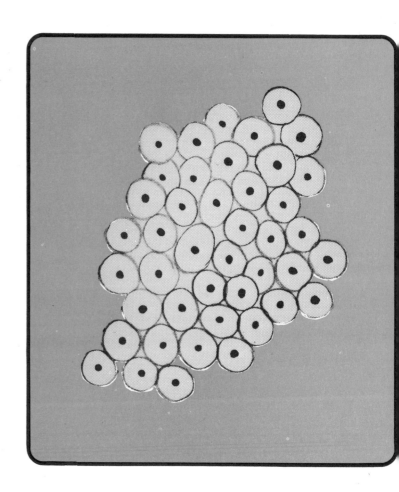

The black eggs develop into an embryo and after about a week the embryo grows a tail. Then slowly, the tiny tadpoles wriggle their way out of the jelly. A tadpole first has frilly gills on each side of its head behind the eyes. Later it develops internal gills like a fish. It sucks water in through the mouth and pumps it out again through its gills, taking out the oxygen it needs.

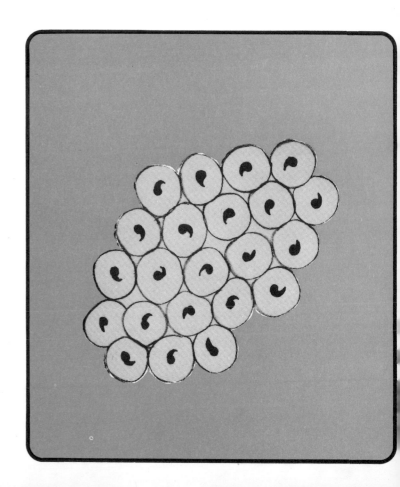

Tadpoles are very tiny when they first hatch. They eat plants in the water, and begin to grow quite quickly. They have four rows of tiny teeth as well as hard jaws which help them to bite their food.

After about four weeks the tadpoles start to grow back legs. At the same time they begin to eat tiny water creatures, as well as plants.

When their back legs have developed they have joints which can bend.

After another four weeks they start to grow front legs. When they have grown their front and back legs, they slowly change shape as they start to grow lungs inside. Later they will use their lungs to breathe air.

While they are changing shape the tadpoles don't eat, so instead they use the food which they have stored up in their tails.

Now they begin to look like frogs as their tails start getting shorter and shorter. They don't want to come out of the water yet, but they use their legs to push themselves along the bottom of the pond, as well as to swim with.

When their tails have completely gone the tiny frogs climb out of the pond and jump away. They are only as long as a fingernail !

It takes three years for the frogs to grow to full size. Adults grow to about 80 millimetres long. Frogs can live until they are 12 years old but not many do, because they have lots of enemies such as rats, herons and hedgehogs, who all like to eat them.

Frogs have a long tongue which is flicked out to catch flies for food. They also like to eat snails, slugs and worms. Frogs can absorb water through their skin.

Kingfisher

Kingfishers are quite small birds, not quite as big as a starling. They look very attractive with the bright blue-green feathers on their backs. They have a long dagger-shaped beak which is used to catch fish.

Usually, kingfishers have their own special perch by the side of the river where they sit watching the water. As soon as they see a fish move under the surface, they dive in and catch it. Then the kingfisher flies back to his perch and bangs the fish's head to stun it, before swallowing it whole !

Kingfishers dig a burrow in the river bank, and at the end of the tunnel they make a nest where the female lays five or six round, white eggs. Both parents help to feed the young kingfishers with minnows and sticklebacks.

Water Vole

Water voles burrow into the banks of slow moving rivers or dykes, and make themselves a snug nest out of grass and reeds. They eat water plants, but if they can't find enough of these they may go off and eat root crops in a nearby field, or strip the bark from young trees. They sit up on their hind legs and use their front ones to hold their food while they nibble it. When they are frightened they dive into the river with a loud *plop* !

Water voles usually have three families each summer, and the babies are naked and completely blind when they are first born. Voles live for about four years. Mistakenly, the water vole is sometimes called a water rat.

Water Shrew

Water shrews also live in holes in river banks, and they have two families a year with about five or six babies each time.

In spite of being so small, they have enormous appetites and will eat small fish and frogs as well as insects. They sometimes search on land for their food and may even kill and eat each other if they are feeling very hungry. As a rule they only live for about a year.

Water shrews wriggle their bodies almost like fish when they swim. There is a fringe of stiff hairs on the underside of the tail which acts as a rudder—a bit like a fishtail in fact.

Water Flowers

All the water plants over the page were found growing in still waters near where I live on the edge of the fens in Cambridgeshire. Except for the bulrush I found them all growing together in one stream.

Bulrush The bulrush stems are used to make baskets and chair seats. They have a very large velvety dark brown seedhead which is beautiful and which people use for decoration in their houses, sometimes after dyeing them bright colours.

Water Plantain The water plantain has small pinky-white flowers growing on a tall stem. It flowers between July and September. At one time people used the leaves as a medicine to cure a disease called dropsy.

Amphibious Persicaria I can't find a common name for this plant, which has lots of tiny pink flowers on a thick stem growing out of the water. It usually flowers between July and September.

Yellow Water Lily This has beautiful bright yellow flowers. It has a thick stem under the water anchoring it to the bottom of the pond. There is a large green seedpod in the middle of the flower, and when this is ripe it floats away from the plant, surrounded by air bubbles. Then it gradually sinks to the bottom, and starts to grow a new plant.

Arrowhead This plant gets its name from the large arrowhead-shaped leaves, which can grow as much as three feet up above the water. It has a very beautiful white, waxy flower which seems to sparkle in the sunlight. The flower centres are purple. This plant has separate male and female flowers, and the male flowers have bigger petals and grow higher up the stem. When the female flowers are over they leave large green prickly fruit which look like burrs.

Water Forget-me-not These plants have little blue flowers, very like the ones we find growing wild or in gardens. They seem to like living equally as well on the bank as actually in the water.

Of course, there were lots of other plants living underneath the water. Most of them send up shoots above the water, into the air. On these there are tiny flowers, which can be pollinated by the wind. Unlike land plants, the water plants use their roots only to anchor them and not to take in water. Some which don't have any roots at all, just float about in the stream.

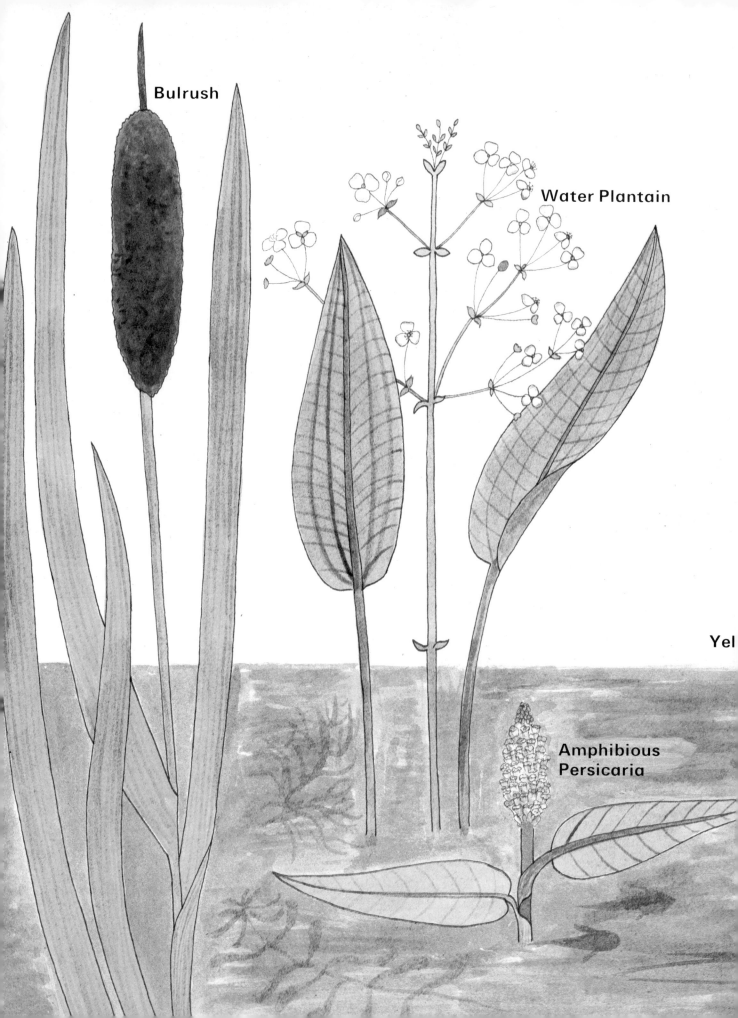

Bulrush

Water Plantain

Yel

Amphibious
Persicaria

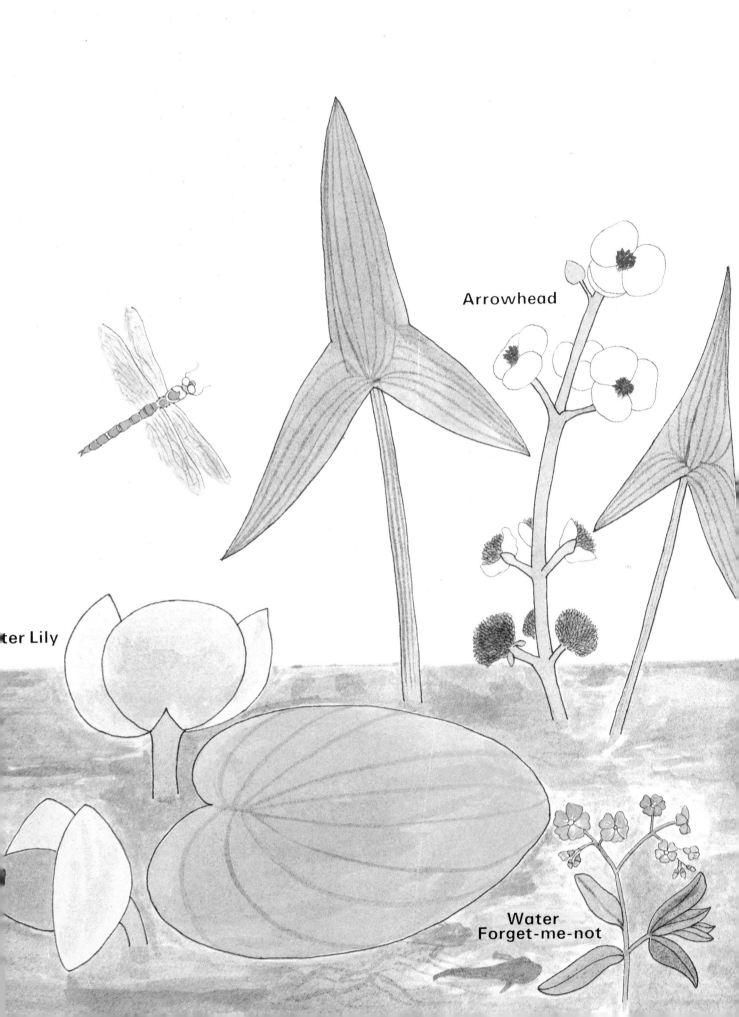

Arrowhead

ter Lily

Water
Forget-me-not

Grasses

If you are in the country, have you ever noticed how many different kinds of grass there are ? How many can you find of the ones shown below, when you next go into a field ? Grass is very important to farmers. Most of the year round, they use it to feed cattle, horses and sheep.

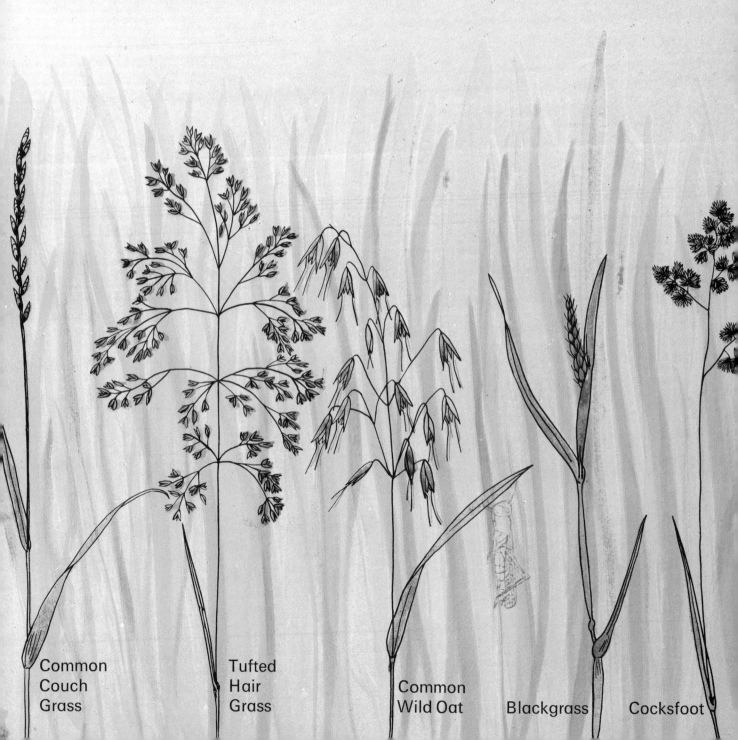

Common Couch Grass

Tufted Hair Grass

Common Wild Oat

Blackgrass

Cocksfoot

Black
Bent
Grass

Annual
Meadow
Grass

Timothy
Grass

Meadow
Fescue

Common
Rye Grass

Grasshopper

Grasshoppers live in fields and meadows. They are difficult to see because they are nearly the same colour as the grass. They eat mainly grass which they chew up with their strong jaws. They have four wings, but they don't usually bother to fly far because they can easily use their long back legs to jump long distances instead. On warm and sunny days the grasshopper sings — a sort of chirruping noise — by rubbing his hind legs against his wings.

In the autumn grasshoppers lay their eggs in a small heap in the grass. The young grasshoppers, called nymphs, hatch out the next spring. They grow up very quickly. Crickets are a bit like grasshoppers, but they come out at night instead of in the day. They make their song, which is shriller than the grasshopper's, by rubbing their wings together.

Crane Fly

Crane flies are often called *Daddy-long-legs* and they live for about a year. Their long legs are no good for running, but they cling on to things when they land. Their legs break off very easily and this helps them to escape if an enemy grabs hold of one in its mouth.

The females have an egg-laying tube at the end of their bodies which they stick into the ground. In the summer, they lay about 100 eggs under the ground. The eggs hatch in the autumn and out come the baby larvae, which are called 'leatherjackets'. They eat the roots of plants and grass, and sometimes do a lot of damage to lawns. After about six months the larvae turn into pupae. The next summer they hatch into adult crane flies. Some adults eat nectar from flowers.

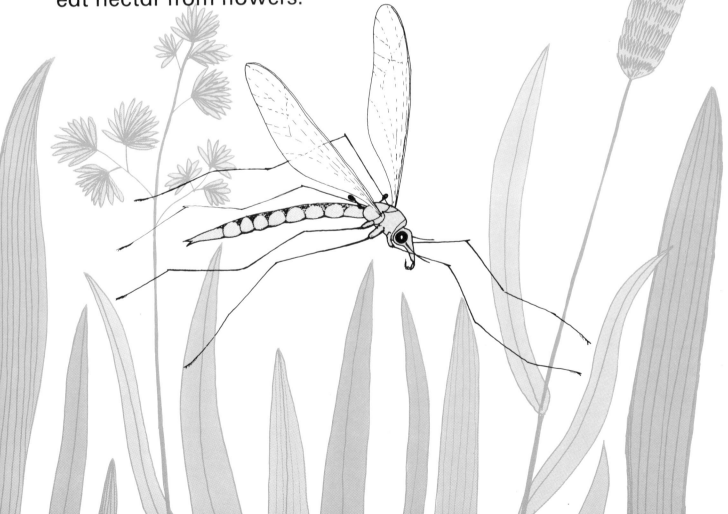

Snail and Slug

Snails and slugs live among plants and under stones. They like damp weather, and when it is very dry or very cold snails are able to close up the doors of their shells. Their eyes are at the end of four stalks, called tentacles. They use their tentacles to smell and touch things as they move along. Snails and slugs both breathe through a hole in their back.

They make a slimy liquid which helps them to cling onto things, as they move along using the flat under-part of their bodies, called a muscular foot. They can easily climb up walls and over stones without falling off.

Slugs and snails use their long tongues, which are covered with hundreds of tiny teeth, to chew up grass and moss for food. The garden snail is a bit of a pest because he likes eating young plants too. They lay eggs in the soil, which hatch out into tiny creatures just like their parents. As baby snails grow up, their shells grow bigger and bigger to fit.

You will quite often find the broken shells of snails lying near a stone path, probably where a thrush has hammered them on the stone, and eaten the snails from inside.

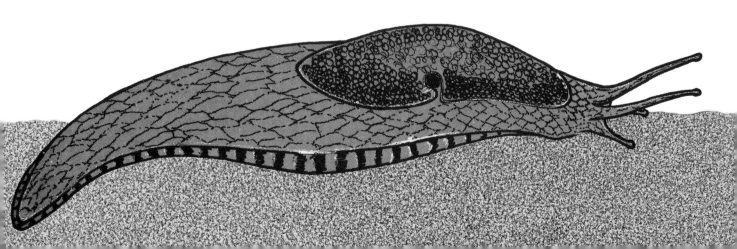

Stoat and Weasel

Stoats are long and slim and perky-looking. They have long whiskers, and a black tip to their tails. They live in tiny caves in stone walls or in holes in the ground. When their time for having babies comes, in late April, they make a nest from dry leaves and grass and the family of three or four is born. The mother stoat feeds them with her own milk and she also brings them dead mice and other small animals to eat. They are very good hunters and they can easily kill a rat.

Stoats

When they grow their winter coats, their fur is sometimes white, except their tails, which makes it easy for them to hide in the snow when they are hunting. People call them ermine when they are white.

Weasels are smaller than stoats and they don't have a black tip to their tails. Unlike stoats, weasels usually have two families each year, with from three to eight babies in each litter.

Badgers and otters belong to the same family as stoats and weasels.

Weasels

Hedgehog

Hedgehogs are a brownish-yellow colour. Their backs are covered in prickles which usually lie flat, and they have furry tummies. If they are frightened, perhaps by a dog, they roll up into a ball and make their prickles stand out to protect themselves.

Hedgehogs eat mainly insects and snails and worms, though they also like fruit. If you are lucky enough to find one in your garden, it will probably like a bowl of bread and milk. They eat a lot of extra food in the autumn to build up their fat which gives them food during their long winter sleep. They hibernate in about December, though a few hedgehogs may come out on one or two sunny days to eat some more food before hurrying back to their nests.

Hedgehogs make nests out of grass and twigs. They usually have two families a year, one in late spring and another in early autumn. They have between three and seven babies at a time, and these are blind at first and have soft spines. The mother hedgehog feeds them with her own milk, and the babies keep squeaking for more. The young hedgehogs soon start playing together, but if one of them strays from the nest, the mother will pick it up by the scruff of the neck and bring it back.

Because of their prickles, hedgehogs can't lick themselves clean, so they usually have lots of fleas. They sometimes make a liquid foam with their mouths which they put on their spines. It is called "anointing" and they may do it to try and get rid of fleas.

Cars are the worst enemy of the hedgehog and very many are killed by being run over. Foxes and badgers both like eating hedgehogs and will attack them even when they are rolled into a ball.

Strangely enough, foxes are cousins to dogs ! They are reddish-brown in colour, with black on the backs of their ears, and they have white markings underneath the body and on the throat. Foxes hunt mainly at night, hiding during the day in holes or burrows, which are called earths. Sometimes one will move into a hole belonging to rabbits or a badger.

Although they don't often make much noise, you can sometimes hear on a winter night a fox making a yapping scream, or barking like a dog. In the spring the female fox or vixen has between three and six cubs. When they are about a month old she takes them out to teach them to hunt and look after themselves. They leave home when they are about three months old. Foxes mostly hunt hares, rabbits and game birds ; they also eat mice and beetles.

In the winter when it is difficult to find food they are brave enough to attack chickens or ducks in poultry yards quite near to houses. They have sometimes been known to carry off young lambs too.

Farmers treat them as pests and they are often hunted by hounds and men on horseback. Foxes are very cunning and to escape being caught they will sometimes jump up into trees to hide, or even swim across water to trick packs of hounds.

Harvest Mouse

Harvest mice are very tiny. Their bodies are only about five or six centimetres long. But they also have a very long tail which they use to help them when they are climbing, by holding onto things with it.

Harvest mice eat insects and seeds. In the winter they make nests under the ground, often under a haystack where they store lots of seeds.

When summer comes, they make a round nest out of shredded corn and grass, which they fix between stalks of wheat, or amongst a bunch of thistles. They have one or two families each summer, with six or seven babies each time.

Woodmouse

The proper name for the woodmouse is *long-tailed field mouse.* Woodmice are very busy and they are very good at jumping and climbing. They dig deep burrows to live in, sometimes several feet deep. They sleep during the daytime in a nest which is made out of shredded grass. They build this at one end of the burrow. They like company and several adult mice sometimes live together in one nest.

As well as berries and grain, which they store near their nests ready for winter, woodmice also eat insects. They have up to six families each year, with four or five babies each time ! But woodmice don't usually live for more than a year because other animals such as badgers, stoats and owls catch them and eat them.

Here are some pictures for you to colour

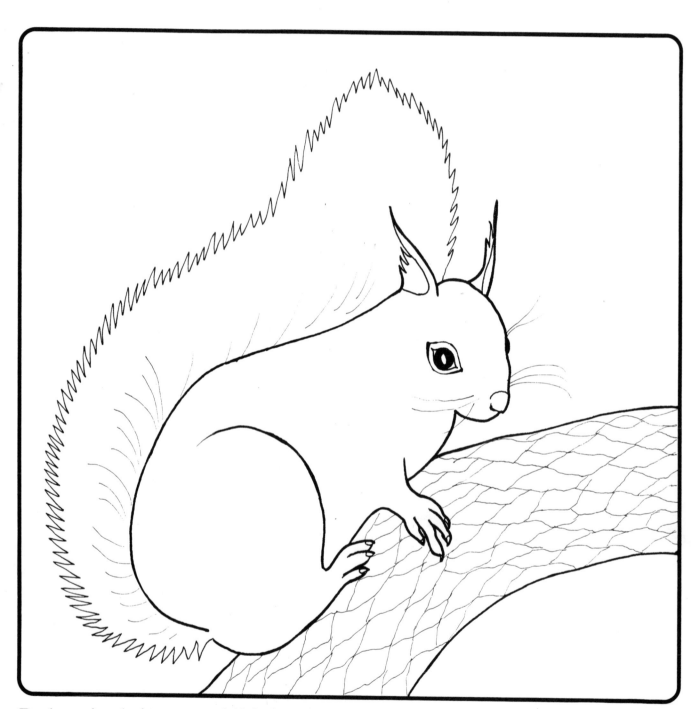

Red squirrels have a reddish-brown
fur coat. They eat nuts and acorns
and they use their paws like hands
to hold their food.

Hedgehogs have black snuffly noses. Their bodies are covered with brown prickles and when they are frightened they roll up into a ball and make their prickles stand out.

The long-tailed field mouse is common all over the
British Isles. He is also called the wood mouse. He is
usually a reddish-brown colour with a grey tummy.

The common toad has a
dry warty skin which is
a greenish colour. Frogs
and toads both start their
lives under the water.

Moles are a dark velvety grey colour. They live under
the ground and they dig passages through the earth with
their strong front legs.

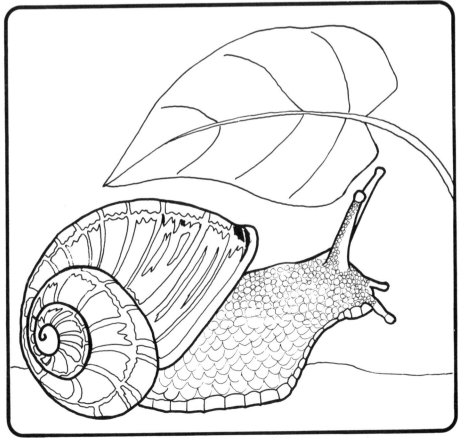

Snails like to live in
damp places, among
plants or under stones.
Some snails have light
and dark brown shells.
Some have yellow and
black, and you may find
some other colours too.
Their bodies are a
greyish-brown colour.

The brown hare is a sandy colour
with an almost white tummy. Hares
are larger than rabbits and behave
differently too. Unlike rabbits they
don't make burrows in the ground
either.

Jays have pinkish-brown bodies
with a blue speckled patch on the
sides of their wings, and some
patches of white. Their tail
feathers are black.

The author would like to thank Brian Gardiner of the Department of Zoology, Cambridge, and Peter Merrin of the Royal Society for the Protection of Birds for their help in vetting the accuracy of this book ; Hilary Abrahams, Veronica Barge and Maureen Galvani for their help with the illustrations, and Celia Henderson who helped to get the book ready for printing.

Swallowtail from egg to chrysalis

Dinosaur Publications

The National Trust
Second Country Book

by Althea

Dinosaur Publications Ltd Over Cambridge England

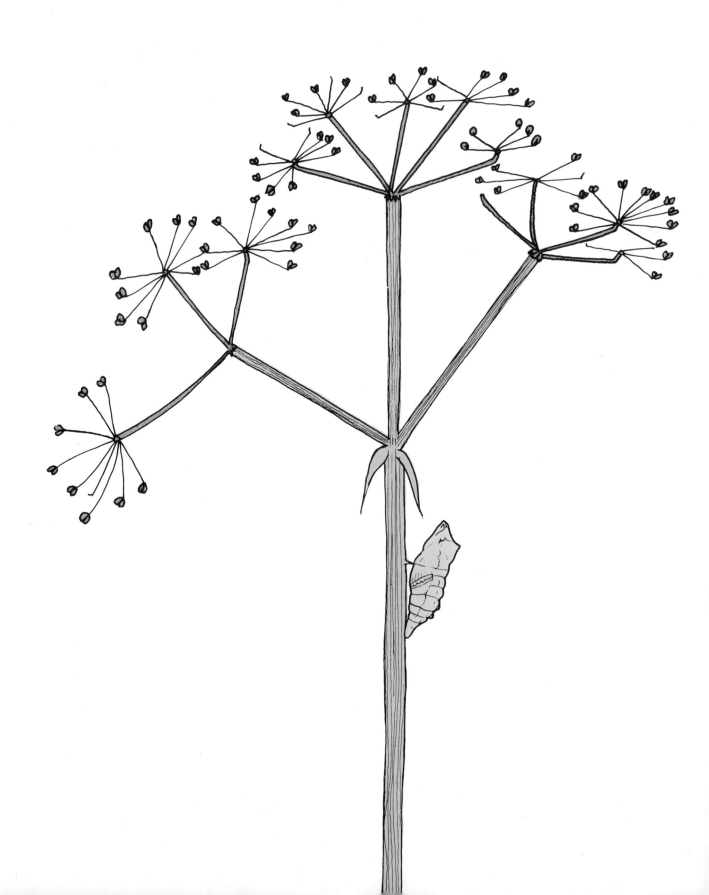

This book is mainly about insects and other invertebrates including butterflies and moths, the plants these animals feed on, and the birds that eat them.

Did you know that up to 500 invertebrates may live on an oak tree? Other trees and shrubs feed different kinds of insects so it's important to have lots of different types of plants and shrubs in our hedgerows.

Althea Braithwaite

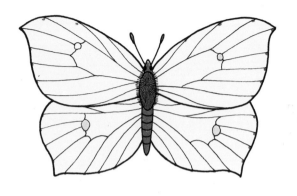
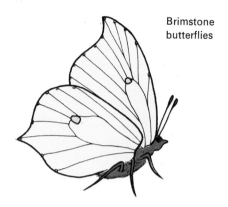

Brimstone
butterflies

Butterflies

Butterflies and moths both belong to the family of insects with scaly wings. The coloured patterns you see on their wings are made out of thousands of small scales, which rub off onto your fingers if you touch them. Each scale is really a tiny, flat bag on a stalk. Some of these are filled with colour, and others have a pattern on the surface, which reflects the light to make an iridescent colour.

Although butterflies and moths are so closely related, there are ways of telling them apart. Butterflies are usually brightly coloured, and only fly during the day. When resting, they sit with their wings closed above their bodies, showing only the duller coloured undersides of their wings. Their antennae, which they use to smell with, are always club-tipped, while a moth's antennae can be finely pointed or feathery.

The word 'butterfly' may have been invented to describe the bright yellow, butter-coloured male Brimstone butterfly pictured here.

The Brimstone is quite common in England and Wales, and can be seen flying along hedgerows and in woods.

The Brimstone is the first butterfly to be seen each year, and for many people it is a symbol of spring. The adult Brimstones hibernate amongst the leaves of ivy or other evergreens, or in sheds or outhouses, and come out on warm days in February or March.

Brimstone egg

Life Cycle of a Butterfly

All butterflies go through four different life stages. After they have mated the female searches for a plant to lay her eggs on. She nearly always chooses the sort of plant that the caterpillars will want to eat when they hatch out. She makes her choice very carefully, using the smell organs in her antennae, head and feet to find out if a plant is suitable. Butterfly eggs can be many different shapes, and usually have tiny raised patterns, which you can see quite well through a magnifying glass.

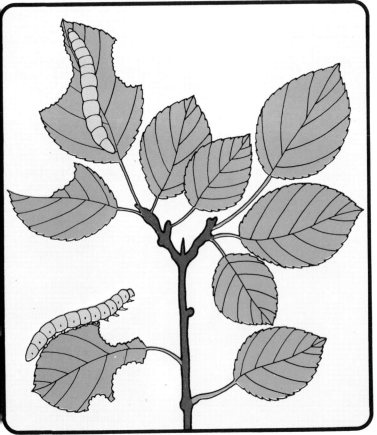

Brimstone caterpillar

After about a week, tiny caterpillars hatch out from the eggs. They start eating immediately, and hardly ever stop. In fact, many caterpillars eat so much that they increase their weight 3,000 times. As the caterpillar grows, its original skin becomes too small, and splits open, revealing a new skin underneath.

A caterpillar may grow four or five new skins, but about a month after it has hatched out, it sheds one last skin and becomes a chrysalis. The chrysalis is usually attached to a twig or leaf, and hangs there, quite still, sometimes looking like a rolled-up leaf itself.

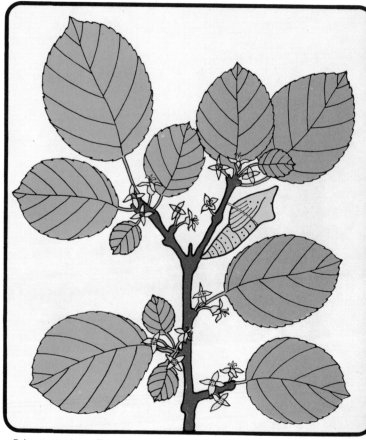

Brimstone chrysalis

When the butterfly is ready the chrysalis splits open down the back and the butterfly struggles out. Its wings are damp and crumpled, so it climbs on to a leaf or twig and waits until they have dried and flattened out in the sun. Then it beats its wings and flies away for the very first time in its life. Its life may last for 10 days or 10 months, depending on its species, but adult butterflies don't grow at all after they have emerged from the chrysalis.

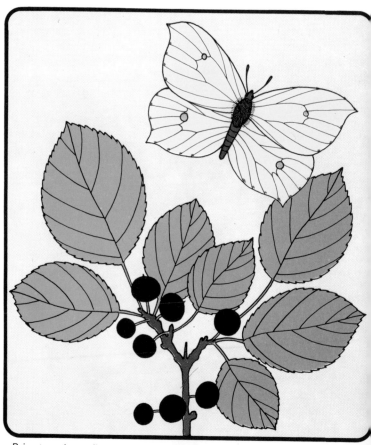

Brimstone butterfly

Swallowtail

The Swallowtail is the largest British butterfly, with a wing span of about 90 mm. It is a strong flier and is very handsome and distinctively marked. This butterfly is very rare now, and is only found in Wicken Fen and the Norfolk Broads. A few sometimes appear in Kent, but these are visitors from the European continent. The Swallowtail lays its eggs on the milk parsley plant which grows in marshy places.

When the caterpillar first hatches it is black and white and looks very much like a bird dropping. But when it is older it changes colour and is very handsome, being a bright green colour, with orange spots on bands of black.

It has an unusual 'Y' shaped organ at the back of its head which sticks up when the caterpillar is alarmed or upset. This organ is orange-coloured and sends out a smell like ripe pineapples to drive attackers away.

A Swallowtail chrysalis is fastened, head upwards, to the stem of a plant by a silken pad at its tail and silk threads round the upper part of its body. It usually spends the winter like this.

You can see the Swallowtail eggs, caterpillar and chrysalis on the title pages of this book.

Meadow Brown

The Meadow Brown used to be one of the commonest butterflies in Britain, but recently there are fewer of them about, and this might be because quite a lot of grassland has been destroyed. They like open fields and are usually seen there between June and September. Meadow Browns have a slow, weak flight, and often seem quite content to sit in the sun rather than fly.

Like all browns, these butterflies have very noticeable 'eye' spots on their wings. These can help to protect them, because if a bird attacks them, it will often go for the 'eyes' which are at the edges of the wings, and so the brown butterflies often escape with only a damaged wing.

Red Admiral

The Red Admiral is quite common in Britain, though it has to fly from North Africa and the South of Europe to get here. You may see it in gardens in England and it likes to feed on rotting fruit such as fallen plums or pears. It also likes buddleia and the flowers of the thistle and ivy. The butterflies arrive in Britain in May or June. The female lays her eggs singly on nettles and when the caterpillars hatch out, they make a tent out of leaves. When they pupate they do so inside a folded leaf, which is a good protection from birds and other enemies. Very few Red Admirals live through the cold British winter, although they sometimes do try to find a warm or sheltered spot to hibernate.

Comma

The Comma is easy to recognise because of the tattered looking edges of its wings, and because of the white 'comma' markings on the underside of its hind wings. It lives in woods, parks and gardens and is usually found in Southern England and Wales.

There are two generations of this butterfly each year, but the first generation only lives for the summer. Adult butterflies of the second generation hibernate in October, clinging to a twig or branch. The dull colouring of their underwings and their ragged shape help to protect them during their hibernation, by making them look like dead leaves.

Common Blue

Most blue butterflies are found in areas with a chalky soil, but the Common Blue can be found in grasslands all over the country. During the day, Common Blues can be seen flying quickly over the meadows, but in the evenings, they gather together amongst the grass stems and rest there, head downwards.

The caterpillars eat birds-foot trefoil. There are two generations each year, and the caterpillars of the second generation hibernate for the winter. In April they wake and spin themselves loose silk cocoons among the leaves of the birds-foot trefoil. Then they turn into chrysalises and each chrysalis rests in its cocoon until the adult butterfly is ready to emerge.

male

female

Adonis Blue

The male Adonis Blue is the most brightly coloured of the British blue butterflies, but the female is mainly brown. They live in the chalk down areas of Southern England and the caterpillars eat horse shoe vetch.

There are two generations each year. The first one appears in May or June and the second in August or September. The second generation caterpillars attach themselves with silk threads to the underneath of the vetch leaves and hibernate for the winter. In the spring they crawl into cracks in the soil and turn into chrysalises.

The caterpillars of the blue butterflies look a bit like wood lice and they have a gland at the back of their necks which makes a sweet fluid. Ants like this sweet fluid, and sometimes 'milk' the caterpillars for it.

Orange Tip

The Orange-tip butterfly belongs to the family of white butterflies. It is very common throughout the whole of the British Isles and can be seen in May and June flying along country lanes and on the edges of woods. The male has very noticeable orange markings on the tips of his forewings. The underneath of the wings of the male and female look dappled green, but if you look closely the markings are actually a mixture of black and yellow spots. This is good camouflage for the butterfly when it rests on plants with its wings closed.

The female Orange-tip lays her eggs among the flowers of the garlic mustard, wild mustard and other wild plants belonging to the cabbage family. The eggs are bright orange and are placed upright on the flower stalks.

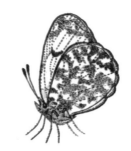

She has to make sure that the eggs are laid quite far apart from each other so that the caterpillars aren't likely to meet. If they do meet the larger caterpillars may eat their smaller brothers and sisters. The Orange-tip caterpillar pupates in the middle of summer and the adult emerges in the late spring.

Silver-washed Fritillary

This is the largest of the Fritillary butterflies and has a wing span of between 72 mm and 76 mm. It gets its name because the underside of the hind wings are streaked with silver. It mainly lives south of the Lake District in woodlands and a great many are found in the New Forest. The butterfly can be seen between July and September, when it feeds on bramble and thistle flowers. The female lays her eggs singly in crevices in the bark of a tree. This is unusual because most other kinds of butterfly lay their eggs on the plant which the caterpillars will eat. After the caterpillars have hatched out they eat their own eggshells and then go into hibernation. When spring comes they drop down from the trees and crawl off to look for dog violets to eat.

Peacock

This butterfly is easy to recognise because of the startling eye markings on its wings. When it is resting the eyes are hidden because the wings are folded together, but if it is disturbed the butterfly quickly opens its wings and displays the eyes. This usually frightens an attacking bird away, because it thinks it has disturbed quite a large animal.

During the winter they sleep in a hollow tree, an outbuilding, or some other sheltered place. In May they lay their eggs on stinging nettles, and when the black spiny caterpillars hatch out they live in groups in a web of silk. Later on the groups split up and the single caterpillars turn into chrysalises.

Painted Lady

The Painted Lady butterfly comes here every year from North Africa. It arrives in May or June and often looks very tattered after its terribly long journey. Soon after they arrive here the females lay their eggs one at a time on thistles or nettles.

The caterpillars hatch out during the summer and feed on these plants. They pupate hanging upside down from the underside of a leaf. The new butterflies come out in late summer and in October most of them fly South. Any that stay behind in this country die because of the cold.

The Painted Lady has a very graceful and swift flight and you can see it gliding for long distances with its wings stretched out.

White Admiral

The White Admiral is a member of the Fritillary family and has a strong graceful flight. It lives in woodlands in Southern England and one can see it flying around bramble blossoms in July and August. Its wings often look a bit tattered, because they get torn on the bramble thorns.

White Admirals lay their eggs on honeysuckle leaves in the shade. The caterpillars, which hatch out a week later, camouflage themselves by sticking bits of leaves on their backs. When autumn comes the caterpillars build a shelter by pulling the edges of a leaf together and tying it to a stem with a thread of silk.

They start feeding again in spring and they pupate in June.

Small Tortoiseshell

The Small Tortoiseshell butterfly is one of our prettiest butterflies. The top side of its wings is very colourful, but the underneath is dark and dull, so that the butterfly is difficult to see when it rests with its wings together.

The Small Tortoiseshell is found all over the British Isles and can often be seen resting on garden flowers, especially buddleia. The females lay their eggs in clusters on the underside of a nettle leaf When the caterpillars hatch out they weave silken webs among the leaves and live and feed together. Later they separate to turn into chrysalises, usually on a twig or a fence.

Marbled White

The Marbled White butterfly likes meadows, wasteland or any open country with long grass. It is found mainly in the South and West of England. In spite of its name, and the patches of white on its wings, this butterfly actually belongs to the family of brown butterflies.

The Marbled White is a rather unusual butterfly because it walks on only four of its six legs. When the female lays her eggs, she drops them at random while flying among the grass. The caterpillar hatches and only eats the shell of its egg before hibernating for the winter. When it wakes up in the spring it eats grass and in July it pupates on the ground among the grass roots.

Grizzled Skipper

Skippers are small butterflies which look a bit like moths because of their size and their hairy bodies. Their wings beat rapidly and they have a quick, darting flight.

The Grizzled Skipper is found in Southern England and Wales and you can see it between April and June, darting amongst the flowers. The female lays her eggs one at a time on the leaves of wild strawberries, brambles and wild raspberries. The caterpillar weaves the leaves of these plants together with silk to make itself a shelter in which to feed. It pupates at the base of the plant in a cocoon made from silk and leaves.

Gatekeeper or Hedge Brown

This butterfly has two names because of the way it behaves. It often flies along hedges where it feeds on bramble blossom and seems to spend some of its time flitting around gates. It is mostly found during July and August in England and Wales. The female Gatekeepers are larger and paler than the males. The caterpillars, which feed until winter, coming out at night to eat grass, hibernate before the cold sets in and then wake up and feed again until they pupate in June.

Flowering Shrubs

There are lots of different kinds of trees and flowering shrubs in our hedgerows. You can guess how old a hedge is by counting the number of different shrubs growing in it. The more varieties there are, the older the hedge is, and each kind of shrub represents roughly a hundred years. Hedges are very important nature reserves, because all sorts of animals, insects and birds live and feed there.

Honeysuckle

Honeysuckle wraps its strong stems clockwise around the stems of other plants. The White Admiral butterfly lays its eggs on Honeysuckle and the caterpillars squeeze themselves down the long tube of the flower so that they can drink the nectar at the bottom.

The sweet scent of the Honeysuckle grows stronger in the evening, and attracts Hawkmoths, which unroll their long hollow tongues to suck up the nectar. In the autumn, this plant bears dark red berries, which are eaten by birds.

Ivy

Ivy, unlike most other plants, flowers in the autumn and bears its berries in the spring. Many different kinds of insects such as wasps, flies, bees and butterflies, feed on the flowers. The nectar makes them feel drunk and drowsy, and if you shake the Ivy, some insects may tumble sleepily out of it. In spring, Blackbirds and Thrushes come to eat the purplish-black berries.

Bees

There are about 250 different kinds of bees in this country. Some of them live all by themselves, and others like to live with lots of other bees in groups called colonies. The best known of these are the Bumble Bee and the Honey Bee.

Bumble Bee

Only the queen Bumble Bees live through the winter. In the spring the queen makes a nest underground and lays about twelve eggs. She covers these with wax and sits on them until they hatch. Soon, grubs come out of the eggs, and she feeds them with a mixture of pollen and honey. In two or three weeks the grubs are fully grown and become the workers. Their job is then to help the queen build the nest, and to feed their younger brothers and sisters.

Honey Bee

Honey Bees are smaller than Bumble Bees. They were known in this country in Roman times. They usually live in wooden hives and are looked after by a bee-keeper. Sometimes a swarm of bees escapes and goes off to nest in a hollow tree somewhere.

Honey Bees stay together all the time. In the summer they are busy storing enough food to feed themselves during the winter. The queen bee lays one egg into each six-sided cell in the comb. The workers collect nectar and pollen and feed it to the larvae. The other bees eat it too.

Towards the end of May, when the hive gets overcrowded, the queen will fly off taking as many as 30,000 bees with her to start a new community. She leaves a new queen to look after the old hive. The bee-keeper waits until the swarm settle somewhere like the branch of a tree, then catches them in a box and takes them to a new hive. Queen bees may go on laying eggs each season for three or four years.

Honey Bees

Spider

Spiders are very useful because they eat lots of flies and other insect pests. They are not insects themselves, and the main difference between them and insects is that spiders have eight legs instead of six. They also have sharp poisoned fangs to capture their food, but British spiders don't hurt people. They can see well with their six or eight eyes. Their feelers, which are quite short, are called palps.

Spiders live in hedges and buildings, and they can all make silk. Some spiders make the silk into webs which they use to trap their food. Many, however, lie in wait and pounce on their prey.

Different kinds of spiders make different patterns of webs. The one shown in our picture is made by a garden spider. He can spin the whole web in less than an hour. The outside framework and the spokes of the wheel-like design are made of a strong double thread which hardens as soon as he spins it. The main spiral is sticky, so that when an insect flies into it he gets caught. The spider then rushes out from his hiding place to poison it. Sometimes he covers the insect with silk, and keeps it for later when he is hungry.

Spiders often lay as many as 200 to 300 eggs in the autumn, and carefully wrap them in a cocoon of silk. They disguise the ball of eggs by attaching pieces of dirt or leaves to it, and hide it in a sheltered place, like a hole in the bark of a tree. The heat from the sun makes the eggs hatch the following spring.

Wasp

Wasps live in nests which they make underground or in outbuildings or attics. Each nest has one queen wasp who lays all the eggs. The queen comes out of her winter sleep in the spring and builds the first cells of the nest herself. The cells are made of paper, which the queen makes by chewing up wood. To begin with the nest is about the size of a golf ball. She lays one egg in each cell and when the baby larvae hatch out, she feeds them on chewed-up caterpillars and insects. The larvae soon change into pupae and then into worker wasps.

The workers build the rest of the nest and help to feed and bring up the rest of the family. By the end of the summer the nest may be about the size of a football, with up to 5,000 workers living in it. It is only when all the eggs have been hatched and all the larvae fed, right at the end of the summer, that they have time to go off to find the honey and jam which they love to eat.

When winter comes all the wasps die except for the new queen wasps who have to find somewhere to sleep until the spring.

Earwig

The common earwig is easy to recognise by its reddish-brown colour and by the pincers at the end of its tail. Earwigs use these pincers for fighting each other. They like eating insects, as well as flower petals and fruit which has fallen from trees.

Earwigs have quite big wings, but they hardly ever use them. After mating, the male and female earwig hibernate together all through the winter in an underground cell. When spring comes the female earwig lays her eggs in the cell. When they hatch she looks after the young earwigs, which are called nymphs, until they grow up.

Centipede

There are lots of different kinds of centipede living in this country, but not all of them have 100 legs, which is what the word centipede means. Some kinds have only 30 legs, while others have as many as 200.

They live in damp, dark places because they don't like the light and come out at night to catch their food. They are helpful to the gardener because they eat slugs and other garden pests, which they kill by using a pair of poisoned claws.

Millipede

The main difference between millipedes and centipedes is that millipedes have four legs on nearly every segment of their body, while centipedes have only two. Millipedes live in damp soil and eat plants or decaying leaves and wood.

Privet

Privet is often used to make garden hedges, but you can also find wild privet in hedgerows. The flowers have a sickly sweet scent which insects like very much, and many butterflies feed on them, including Red Admirals, Peacocks and Small Tortoiseshells. The larvae of the Privet Hawk Moth feed on privet leaves, too.

Dog Rose

The Dog Rose has flowers of deep pink to almost white. They are faintly scented and flower from June until August. In autumn, the red berries brighten up the bare hedges, and provide food for birds belonging to the Thrush family — including winter visitors like the Redwing and Fieldfare. Rosehips are full of vitamin C, and are used to make rosehip syrup and rosehip wine.

Blackbird

Female Blackbirds usually lay three, four or five eggs, and then sit on them to hatch them. When the baby birds hatch out, both parents help to feed them, and keep the nest clean by removing the babies' droppings. The young birds leave the nest when they are two weeks old, but the parents go on feeding them on the ground for another three weeks.

The same pairs of Blackbirds often meet again each spring, even though the male and female may have spent the winter apart. Each pair settles down on a territory and the female Blackbird builds a nest in the middle of it. The male goes out with her to look for nesting materials and he protects her from approaches by other Blackbirds.

Blackbirds like eating fruit such as raspberries and hawthorn berries, and they also hunt for insects and worms. When catching worms they stand very still, and watch and listen carefully. They can hear the worms moving under the ground, and as soon as they see the tip of a worm appear, they grab it with their beaks, drag it out, and gobble it up.

Thrush

The Song Thrush likes to eat snails as well as worms and insects. He usually has a special stone called an anvil stone and when he finds a snail he picks it up in his beak and beats it against the stone until the shell breaks. So if you find a stone with lots of broken snail shells nearby you can be pretty sure the stone belongs to a Thrush.

Song Thrushes nest quite early in the year, and have two or three families each year. They line their nests with rotten wood and dung to make them very water tight. After a rainstorm the Thrush sometimes comes back and finds the nest full of water. The female lays four or five shining blue eggs covered with black spots. She sits on the nest until they hatch and then both parents help to feed the hungry babies.

Cuckoo

Cuckoos come back to this country in the spring, after spending the winter in Africa. The cocks call 'cuckoo' to tell everyone they have arrived, and each year different people get excited and write to the newspapers claiming they have heard the first cuckoo.

A Cuckoo never builds a nest of its own. Instead, the hen uses all her energy searching for the nests of other birds such as Robins, Meadow-pipits, or Pied Wagtails in which she lays her eggs. Each Cuckoo hen seems to prefer the nest of one particular kind of bird and she tries to lay all her eggs, one in each nest, with one species. She has to find a nest where the eggs have only just been laid. Then, when both parents are away, she flies up and takes one of the eggs from the nest, and, cleverly balancing on the edge so as not to break the other eggs, she carefully lays one of her own into the nest.

A bird seeing a Cuckoo near its nest will fight to chase it away, but if a Cuckoo manages to lay her egg, the other bird will hatch it and look after the young Cuckoo afterwards. A baby Cuckoo is extremely greedy and soon grows very big. It will push the other babies out of the nest, and soon its new parents are left with only one enormous bird to bring up.

Yellowhammer

Yellowhammers belong to the Bunting family, and are sometimes called Yellow Buntings. They live in hedgerows and can often be heard singing a song which sounds like 'little-bit-of-bread-and-no-cheese'. They make their nests out of dry grasses low down in hedges or on the ground.

These birds are sometimes called 'Writing Larks' because their eggs are a dirty white colour and covered with dark lines and squiggles which look almost like writing. The hen birds have two families of between two and five babies which both parents help to feed.

In the summer Yellowhammers feed on insects and small animals. They also like blackberries and other fruits, and in winter they flock together with different birds to eat the grain they find in farmyards and stubble fields.

Goldfinch

The Goldfinch is very colourful and easy to recognise from the golden yellow bar on its black wings. This bar helps them to recognise each other when they fly together in flocks.

The female builds a small compact nest usually in the branches of a fruit tree. They have two families each year, and the female sits on the eggs to keep them warm, while the male brings her food. She has a brown back so she is difficult to see from above while she is sitting on the nest.

When the five or six babies hatch both parents are kept busy feeding them on insects and larvae. Later when they grow up their main food is seeds from thistles, knapweed, groundsel and other plants.

Wren

The Wren is one of the smallest British birds and because of its short, turned-up tail it is very easy to recognise. The cock Wren builds several different nests, which are ball-shaped with a small entrance hole in the side. The cock then finds a mate, and takes her round to see his nests. When she has chosen the one she likes best, she lines it with soft feathers to make it comfortable. Then she sits inside and lays at least five eggs. Some wrens have been known to lay as many as fourteen eggs.

After the babies hatch out, the parents are kept very busy feeding them and keeping the nest clean. When the young birds leave the nest, the parents go on caring for them, and they stay in their parents' territory until they are quite big.

In the winter when food is scarce, territories become less important to most birds. Sometimes lots of Wrens huddle together, sitting on top of each other in a small hole so that they keep warm during the cold weather – as many as fifty have been known to roost together in a single nesting box.

Bramble

Brambles send their long shoots sprawling all over some hedgerows. In summer, butterflies such as the Hedge Brown, Meadow Brown, White Admiral and Silver Washed Fritillary feed on the flowers. When the blackberries are ripe many different insects and birds like to eat them.

When the berries become mushy, Comma and Red Admiral butterflies suck up the juice. Spiders spin their webs among the leaves, to catch any unwary flies which are attracted to the fruit.

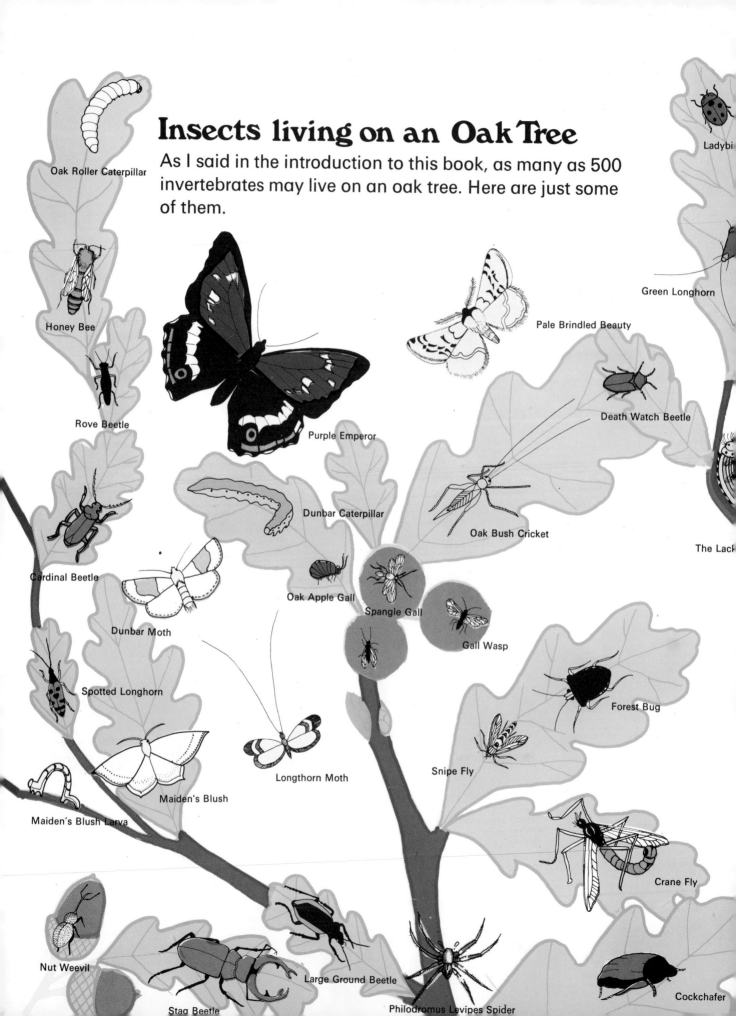

Insects living on an Oak Tree

As I said in the introduction to this book, as many as 500 invertebrates may live on an oak tree. Here are just some of them.

Oak Roller Caterpillar

Honey Bee

Rove Beetle

Cardinal Beetle

Dunbar Moth

Spotted Longhorn

Maiden's Blush

Maiden's Blush Larva

Nut Weevil

Stag Beetle

Purple Emperor

Dunbar Caterpillar

Oak Apple Gall

Spangle Gall

Gall Wasp

Longthorn Moth

Large Ground Beetle

Philodromus Levipes Spider

Pale Brindled Beauty

Death Watch Beetle

Oak Bush Cricket

The Lack

Snipe Fly

Forest Bug

Crane Fly

Ladybi

Green Longhorn

Cockchafer

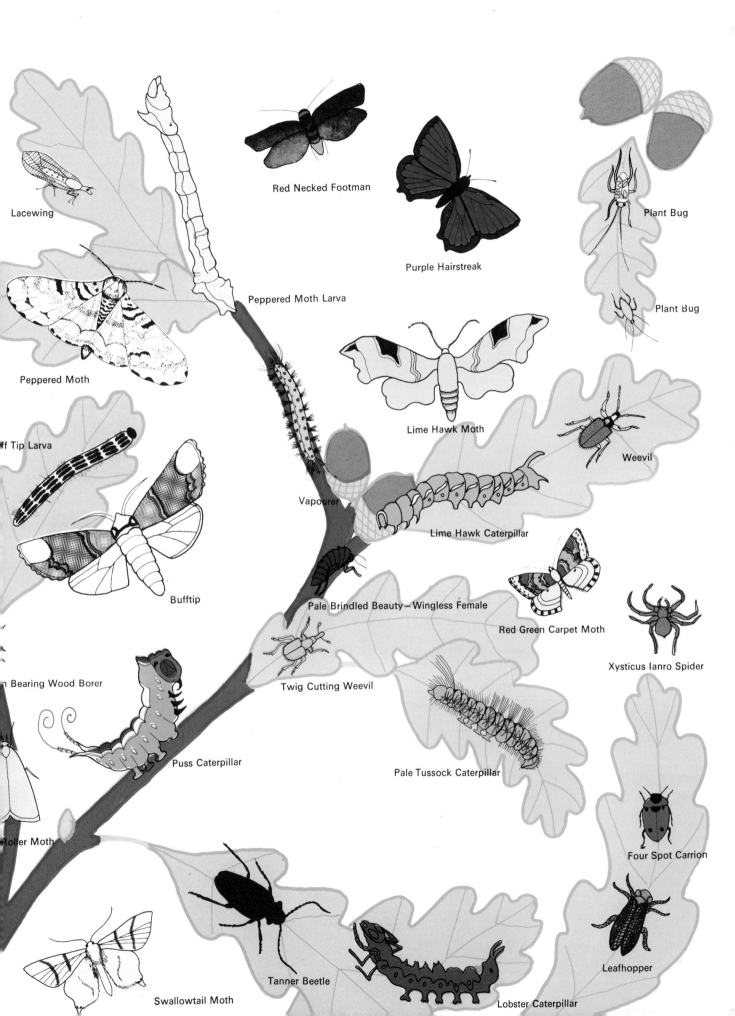

Lacewing

Red Necked Footman

Purple Hairstreak

Plant Bug

Plant Bug

Peppered Moth Larva

Peppered Moth

ff Tip Larva

Lime Hawk Moth

Weevil

Vapourer

Lime Hawk Caterpillar

Bufftip

Red Green Carpet Moth

Pale Brindled Beauty – Wingless Female

Xysticus Ianro Spider

n Bearing Wood Borer

Twig Cutting Weevil

Puss Caterpillar

Pale Tussock Caterpillar

Four Spot Carrion

Roller Moth

Leafhopper

Swallowtail Moth

Tanner Beetle

Lobster Caterpillar

Flowers

Sweet Violet

You can find tiny wild violets growing in all sorts of shady spots during the early spring. They are of different colours varying from deep purple to pure white, and the smell of the sweet violet is lovely. Their cousins, cultivated violets, are sometimes covered with sugar and used as cake decorations as well as being used to make perfumes.

The dark lines on the lower petal of the violet are called *honey guides* because they show bees where the nectar is, which they need to make honey.

Sweet Violet

Wood Violet

Marsh Violet

Celandine

Lesser celandines, which funnily enough, are not related to the greater celandines, come into flower at the same time as the violet. Growing in damp spots under shady trees, the plants spread very quickly. The flowers look very shiny and bright against their green leaves.

Lesser Celandine

Greater Celandine

Primrose

Primroses are another beautiful spring flower. They get their name from *primus* which, in Latin, means 'first.' At one time people used them to make wine, but you need large quantities of flower heads so it would be a shame to do this now.

Snowdrop

Aconite

Primrose

Cowslip

Cowslip flowers grow on the end of a long stalk about six to eight inches high. They flower a little later than primroses. They have a sweet smell and the bees are very fond of the nectar for making honey. Cowslip leaves look very like primrose leaves.

In the Middle Ages people thought that cowslips had marvellous powers as medicine. Ointment made from the flowers was supposed to cure all spots and wrinkles, and liquid medicine would end all other sorts of pains and sickness !

Buttercup

Yarrow

owslip

Foxglove

Sorrell

Mullein

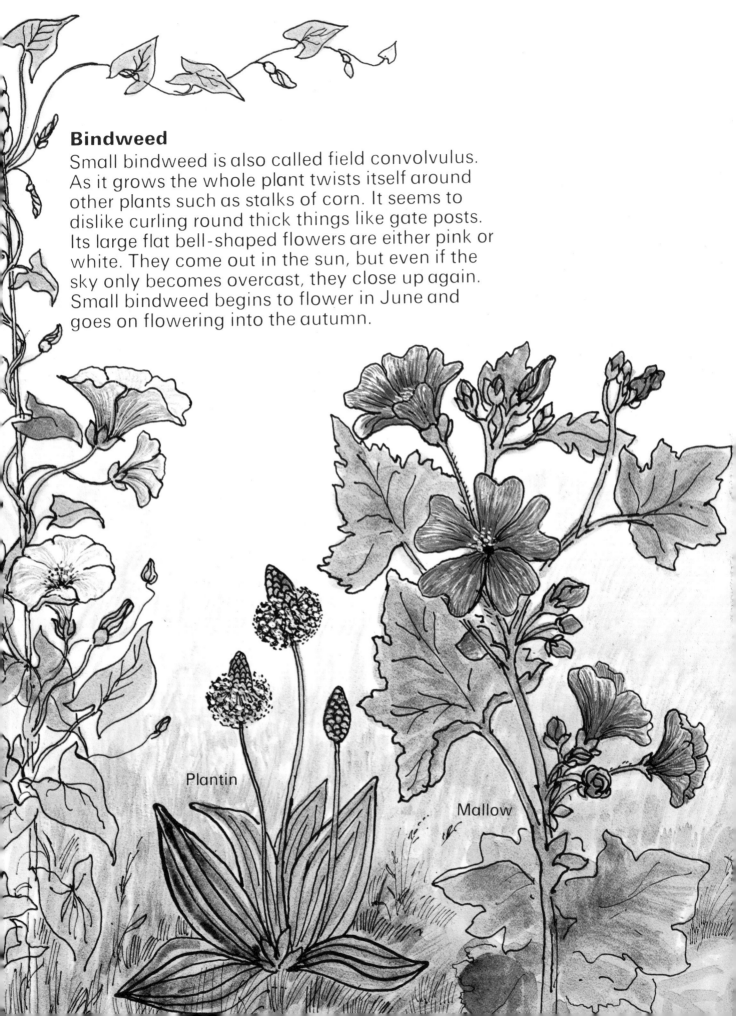

Bindweed

Small bindweed is also called field convolvulus. As it grows the whole plant twists itself around other plants such as stalks of corn. It seems to dislike curling round thick things like gate posts. Its large flat bell-shaped flowers are either pink or white. They come out in the sun, but even if the sky only becomes overcast, they close up again. Small bindweed begins to flower in June and goes on flowering into the autumn.

Plantin

Mallow

Moths

It is usually easy to tell the difference between a moth and a butterfly. Unlike butterflies, moths mostly fly at night time. They don't have such brightly coloured wings as most butterflies and they often rest with their wings flat instead of closed together. Their antennae are either finely pointed or feathery. Very few moths live for more than a few weeks and many of them are quite tiny with a wing span of between 5 mm and 25 mm. There are large ones too, such as the great Death's Head Hawkmoth which is the largest British insect, with a wing span of about 140 mm.

Some moths have tiny bristles on their hind wings which catch on to a sort of loop on their front wings so that they can hook the wings together when they want to fly. Then the front and hind wings move as if they were just a single wing.

A moth's life, from egg to adult, is very like that of a butterfly, but unlike butterflies, many moth larvae spin a cocoon or bury themselves a few inches underground when they pupate.

Square Spot Rustic
The Square Spot Rustic is very common in most parts of Britain. They come to lighted windows at night and are often eaten by bats, who catch them as they fly. During the day, you are quite likely to find them resting behind curtains – even in big cities like London.

This is the sort of dull-coloured creature that most people think of when they talk about moths, but look on the next few pages and see some of the other fascinating moths there are.

Garden Tiger

The Garden Tiger Moth has a wingspan of between 65 mm and 75 mm and because of its size and bright colour, it is sometimes mistaken for a butterfly. The female lays her eggs in batches on the leaves of the plants the caterpillars like to eat, such as docks, dandelions and dead nettles. The caterpillars are hairy 'woolly bears'. The hairs are irritating and this stops all birds except cuckoos from eating them.

When fully grown the caterpillars spin a cocoon out of a mixture of silk and their own hairs and pupate in vegetation on the ground.

The Garden Tiger flies at night, but it doesn't bother to hide during the day. It rests with its forewings folded over its hindwings. If it is frightened, it sticks out its antennae, unfolds its wings to show the bright red and black hindwings and raises a fringe of red hairs just behind its neck. If this doesn't frighten off an attacking bird, it should do, because it happens that the Garden Tiger is also poisonous. Some insects which are not really poisonous protect themselves by using the same bright colours.

Eyed Hawk Moth

The Eyed Hawk Moth is quite common in Southern England. It looks like a dead leaf when it is resting on a tree or fence, with its front wings folded over the hind ones. When it is disturbed it displays its hindwings, which have large blue eyespots, and this makes it look like the face of a large animal.

Death's Head Hawkmoth

This is the largest British moth, and also the largest insect found in this country. It can't survive the cold during the British winter and migrates here from the European continent every spring. It gets its name from the yellow markings on its back, which look very like a human skull.

When it is alarmed this moth makes a strange squeaking noise. To do this, it forces air out through its short proboscis, which is the hollow tongue it uses to suck nectar from flowers.

Puss Moth

The Puss Moth can be found in most parts of Britain. It has a thick, furry body, like a fluffy cat. The female lays her eggs on a willow tree, and the reddish colour of the eggs helps to disguise them as disease spots on the leaves.

The caterpillar is black when it hatches, but later turns green and purple, and looks like a leaf. When attacked, it waves its forked tail and spurts out formic acid. Then it rears its head and displays red markings and two black 'eye' spots, to frighten its attacker.

In September, when it is fully grown, the caterpillar crawls into a crevice in the bark of a tree. There it makes a very strong, hard cocoon from silk and pieces of chewed-up wood and inside this shelter, it turns into a pupa. The next spring the adult moth has to force its way out of the hard cocoon. It puts some caustic fluid on the inside of the cocoon, to soften it, and then it cuts a hole using part of the pupa case, which is still sticking to its head, as a knife.

Ruby Tiger

The Ruby Tiger is often seen in open woodland, heaths, moors and in marshy fields and grassy places. It flies mostly at night. The females lay large batches of eggs on heather, dock and dandelions. There are two generations, one in April to June and another in July to September.

The second generation of caterpillars hibernate, and then pupate early in the spring. The pupae, which are black with rings of yellow, lie in cocoons of brown silk among plants on the ground.

Burnet Moth

Burnet moths live in colonies, and fly around during the day. Their colours warn birds not to try to eat them, because like many brightly-coloured moths they have a nasty taste. If they are attacked by birds they frighten them off by producing a drop of yellow fluid containing prussic acid, which makes the birds feel sick.

The colour of the Burnet moth's wings varies according to the angle at which they reflect the light. This is because the scales on the moth's wing are not actually coloured, but have a raised pattern which reflects the light in such a way that they look green, blue or black according to how the light strikes them.

The female Burnet moth lays batches of yellow eggs on clover or birds' foot trefoil. The larvae make papery cocoons at the tops of grass stems.

There are seven different species of this moth. The Six Spot Burnet is the most common.

Red Underwing

The Red Underwing is one of the largest British moths, measuring up to 90 mm. It has beautiful red and black hindwings, which are kept hidden under its dull, brown forewings when it is resting. If it is disturbed, the moth flies off showing its red wings and the enemy chases the red markings. Suddenly, the moth settles on a branch, folds its wings, and because its coloured hindwings are hidden it seems to disappear.

The Red Underwing flies at night in August and September. The females lay their eggs singly on the bark of poplar or willow trees. The caterpillars eat at night, and make silk cocoons among the leaves.

Peppered Moth

The Peppered Moth feeds on oaks and other trees. Its wings are peppered with black spots. In industrial areas darker varieties of the Peppered Moth have appeared over recent years. The usual white and black marking is a good camouflage when the moth rests against a lichen covered tree trunk, but if the tree is blackened with soot, the moth is too easy to see and more likely to be eaten by birds. The darker moths are well hidden on blackened bark.

The Peppered Moth caterpillar has a long body with six pairs of legs at the front, two pairs of claspers at the back, and a long section in the middle with no legs at all. As the caterpillar moves, it loops this middle part of its body upwards, as if measuring the thing it is walking on.

Cinnabar

The Cinnabar Moth is found all over the British Isles except Northern Scotland. It can often be seen on waste ground in large cities, where ragwort grows. It flies at night and during the day. Both adults and caterpillars use bright colours as protection. The colours are to warn the birds and other enemies that they are not worth eating because of their nasty taste.

The female Cinnabar lays batches of yellow eggs on ragwort, groundsel or coltsfoot. Orange caterpillars with black bands hatch out and feed together in groups. As they feed, they strip all the leaves off these plants and this prevents ragwort from spreading as much as it would otherwise do.

Humming-bird Hawk Moth

The best place to look for the Humming-bird Hawk Moth is in parks and gardens where there are lots of flowers. This moth looks very like a humming bird as it hovers over a flower, quickly beating its wings. It likes sucking the nectar from honeysuckle, which has an especially strong scent at night.

In some years, there may be quite a lot of Humming-bird Hawk Moths in Britain, but in other years there are hardly any. They come from Southern Europe, and start arriving in June, often flying a hundred miles a day. Sometimes they breed here – laying their eggs on the bedstraw plant which is the caterpillar's food. When winter comes most of these moths die from the cold.

Elephant Hawk Moth

This moth flies at night time, and hovers over flowers, sucking up nectar through the long proboscis at the front of its head. It is called 'elephant' because the caterpillar, when it is disturbed, stretches its head and neck rather like an elephant's trunk. Then it draws back its head, and the neck swells up, displaying two large eye-spots to frighten off attackers.

During late summer, the caterpillars feed at night on rose-bay and great willow herb and fuschia. Rose-bay willow herb grows in empty spaces like demolition sites and railway cuttings, and the Elephant Hawk Moth can be found in most parts of England, Wales and Ireland, where this plant grows.

White Ermine

The forewings of the White Ermine moth are speckled, and look like an ermine cloak. It doesn't fly during the day, but can sometimes be seen in the daytime, resting on a tree or fence.

The caterpillars have long fur, which is dark brown or black, with a line of orange down the back. They particularly like dandelion and dock leaves to eat, but in September they leave their food plants, because they have an urge to hibernate. You can sometimes see them in groups on the march, looking for a comfortable place to spin their cocoons. They spend the winter among dead leaves, on the ground. In June the adult moth comes out.

Emperor

The Emperor moth has prominent eye-spots on its front and hind wings. The male flies during the day, but the female only flies at night. During the day, she sits among plants and gives out a scent which attracts the male. A male Emperor moth has large feathery antennae, which pick up the scent of any female looking for a mate, from as far away as half a mile. After mating, the female lays eggs on heather or brambles.

The Emperor is the only British member of the Silk Moth family – though its coarse brown silk can't be used for making material. The cocoon which the larva spins has a pointed end with a ring of spikes around it. The points of the spikes meet, but they open if pushed from inside, so that the caterpillar can get out but enemies can't get in.

The Drinker

The Drinker moth belongs to a family of moths called Eggars. The adults of the Eggar family have no proper mouths, but as the adult only lives for about a week it doesn't need to feed at all.

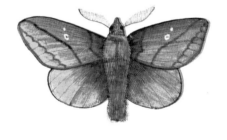

The Drinker lives all over Britain and is found in open country, mostly in damp, marshy places. The eggs are laid in groups on the stem of reeds, grass or sedge. The baby larvae like to drink dew and raindrops. They hibernate from October to April, then carry on feeding, and pupate in June. The pupa is wrapped in a long, brown, papery cocoon, which is fixed to the stem of a reed or grass.

Rose Bay Willow Herb

Corn Chamomile

Ladies Sma

Dandelion

The name *dandelion* means 'lion's teeth.'
Dandelions flower most of the year round and have
a nasty habit of growing in the middle of people's
lawns ! They are very difficult to get rid of because
their exceptionally long root goes deep into the
ground and is difficult to dig out completely.

One name for the dandelion was 'pee-in-the-bed'
because if you picked a dandelion you were
supposed to wet your bed that night ! The
seed-head is sometimes called a clock, because
people pretend that by blowing the clock and
counting until all the seeds have gone they can
tell the time. This is not very popular if you do it
near someone's lawn.

Dandelion roots are sometimes roasted and used as
coffee, or cooked and used as a vegetable, and
some people say the leaves are good in salad.

Red Campion

Shepherds Purse

Ragged Robin

Red and White Clover

Clover flowers are dark pink or white, and they smell beautiful. Bees are particularly fond of the nectar from clover for honey-making. Most clover leaves are made up of three leaflets, but it is supposed to be very lucky if you find one with four !

Farmers cultivate a different sort of clover for use as a cattle food. They also grow it to plough back into the earth, because the leaves of clover contain a lot of nitrogen which helps to improve the soil.

White Clover